Alfred Orage

Nietzsche

The Dionysian Spirit of the Age

with a new introduction by
Michael Paraskos

The **Orage** Press
2013

Originally published in hardback in 1906
by T.N. Foulis. Completely reset and republished
in paperback with a new introduction
by Michael Paraskos in 2013 by the Orage Press.

The Orage Press
16A Heaton Road
Mitcham
Surrey
CR4 2BU
England

ISBN: 978 0 9565802 5 2

Printed by Lightningsource

INTRODUCTION

Alfred Orage and the Modernist Spirit of the Age by Michael Paraskos

Even before he was cold in his grave British critics were dismissing Friedrich Wilhelm Nietzsche's influence in Britain as negligible. In the London *Times* newspaper in 1900 the obituary writer noted that being revolutionary Nietzsche's philosophy was altogether impractical, and that 'his works were certainly not taken very seriously in England.'[1]

Judy, a rival to the satirical magazine *Punch*, suggested that the preaching of 'the mad professor' Nietzsche takes the form of 'three sealed books to English readers',[2] It advised people to accept the judgement on Nietzsche of Max Nordau, a popular writer of the time who specialised in prophesying global doom and gloom. In his widely read book *Degeneration* Nordau said of Nietzsche: 'This unhappy lunatic has been put forward as a "philosopher", and his drivel put forward as a "system" –this man whose

---

[1] 'Professor Nietzsche' in *The Times*, 27 August 1900, p.4

[2] 'Scribes and Pharisees: Our Literary Log' in *Judy: The London Serio-Comic Journal*, 12 September 1900, p.442

scribbling is one single loud divagation, in whose writings madness shrieks out from every line!'[3]

Not all judgements were so sneering. *The Athenæum* described Nietzsche as a 'brilliant writer, but unhappy philosopher', although even it goes on to suggest that he only had limited appeal in Britain. 'Such reputation as Nietzsche possessed in this country,' *The Athenæum's* correspondent wrote, 'is the growth only of the last decade.' Even then it was little more than 'a fashionable substitute for political or theological scandal.'[4]

This might suggest we agree with the obituary writer in *The Speaker* magazine that in Britain Nietzsche 'is likely to have less than justice done him.'[5] The view from mainstream publications in Britain was that Nietzsche represented an interesting, if somewhat dotty, form of philosophy that will pass into well-deserved oblivion.

With the benefit of hindsight it is easy to dismiss these judgements, but even at the time a small number of journals did recognise the impact of Nietzsche was greater than many members of the British bourgeoisie might have imagined or hoped. R. Peggio writing in *The Musical Standard* noted that Nietzsche's ideas 'have had more influence in

---

[3] Max Nordau, *Degeneration* (London : William Heinemann, 1895) p.468-9

[4] 'Friedrich Nietzsche' in *The Athenaeum*, 1 September 1900, p.281

[5] 'Friedrich Nietzsche' in *The Speaker*, 1 September 1900, p. 586

England than most people will admit.' With prescience Peggio recognised that, 'they have influenced many of the younger men –and sometimes not for good– and have become absorbed as part of the stock in trade of modern thinkers.'[6]

It was one of those younger men, Alfred Orage, who came to write this book, *Friedrich Nietzsche: The Dionysian Spirit of the Age.* Alongside Nietzsche's original works, a convincing argument can be made that this little book was one of the most important texts in the development of a specifically Nietzschean strand of modernist thinking in the twentieth century, at least in the English speaking world. Yet it is also a book that is almost wholly forgotten.

* * *

Alfred Orage was born in the village of Dacre, in Yorkshire in the north of England in 1873. His mother was widowed when Orage was still a child and in penury they moved south to stay with family in the Huntingdonshire village of Fenstanton. There Orage showed promise at school, but the family's poverty meant help from a local squire was required for him to complete his education. Orage attended the teacher training college in Abingdon,

---

[6] R. Peggio. 'Rambling Reflections' in *The Musical Standard,* 1 September 1900, p.133

Oxfordshire in 1892.[7] The following year, after graduation, he returned to Yorkshire to become a schoolteacher in Leeds, working in the areas of Cross Green and the Leylands. Both were slums, the first dominated by Irish working class labourers, the second by Jewish immigrants fleeing pogroms in eastern Europe.

In 1902 Orage began teaching at Roundhay Road School, in a slightly higher social class area some two miles north of the Leylands. Here he remained until the start of the Christmas holidays in December 1905, when he was granted a six month sabbatical to write a book. It was to be the end of his life as a schoolteacher,[8] and the book he produced was this one, *Friedrich Nietzsche: The Dionysian Spirit of the Age*. It was published in 1906 by the somewhat eccentric Scottish publisher Thomas Noble Foulis as part of a series, known collectively as 'The Spirit of the Age'. Other titles in the series included Eve Blantyre Simpson on Robert Louis Stevenson and Haldane MacFall on James Abbott McNeill Whistler. Foulis was vehemently opposed to the the increasing use of mechanical processes in the printing industry, and sought to produce books which come close to the work of the artisan bookbinders inspired by

---

[7] Tom Gibbons, *Rooms in the Darwin Hotel* (Nedlands: University of Western Australia Press, 1973) p. 98

[8] Tom Steele, *Alfred Orage and the Leeds Arts Club 1893-1923* (Mitcham: Orage Press, 2009), pp.26-8

William Morris and the Arts and Crafts Movement. It was an approach that led Foulis into bankruptcy, but it also associated his press with artists, many of whom produced decorations for his books. This included Jessie Marion King, William Russell Flint, Frank Brangwyn and Frederick Cayley Robinson, all leading avant-garde artists in turn of the century Britain.[9] This suggests Orage intended his book on Nietzsche to be associated with a particular artistic group in British society.

The book opens with an extraordinarily exuberant statement from Orage: 'Friedrich Nietzsche is the greatest European event since Goethe.' As one of Orage's biographers, Wallace Martin, has suggested for Orage the discovery of Nietzsche was not a dry or academic gratification, it was an emotional event.[10] This is undoubtedly true, although as we shall see, Orage was not uncritical of any of his influences. But in the context of his book on Nietzsche Orage's extravagant claim was also politically astute. As we have heard, mainstream society viewed Nietzsche as an irrelevance or even a dangerous madman. By linking Nietzsche to Goethe Orage not only showed his own diverse intellectual affiliations but created a bridge to encourage this

---

[9] See Ian Elfick, *T.N. Foulis: The History and Bibliography of an Edinburgh Publishing House* (Delaware: Oak Knoll Press,1998)

[10] Wallace Martin, *Orage as Critic* (London: Routledge, 1974) pp.9-10

skeptical Edwardian readership that if they admired Goethe they might also admire Nietzsche. In fact Orage went further than this by suggesting that Nietzsche stands in the same tradition as the British poet and artist William Blake. (p.24) Orage undoubtedly believed this, but in the absence of any in depth comparisons in the book it should also be read as a rhetorical device to allow Orage to entreat his audience to recognise Nietzsche's greatness.

One of the features of Orage's prose is its clarity. As the initial linking of Nietzsche with familiar figures such as Goethe and Blake shows, *Friedrich Nietzsche: The Dionysian Spirit of the Age* is a kind of primer for a general readership. Just taking one chapter as an example, 'Apollo or Dionysos?', we can see how Orage takes the reader on a step by step journey through ancient Greek history, onto the differences between Apollo and Dionysos and ending with the resolution of those differences. This literary style was to hold Orage in good stead later on when be became co-owner and editor of the hugely influential weekly journal *The New Age*. There he acted as a kind of mentor to a number of writers including Kathleen Mansfield and Herbert Read. Mansfield's comment on Orage was that he taught her to write, a view echoed by Read when he admitted: 'I worshipped Orage when I first came to

London and began writing under his tutelage.'[11]

What Mansfield and Read took from Orage was a vigorous, often declamatory, writing style that avoided falling into the trap of preaching. We can see this in *Friedrich Nietzsche: The Dionysian Spirit of the Age*. In the chapter 'Apollo or Dionysos?' Orage sets out the groundwork for understanding Nietzsche, but at no point does he make that understanding seem like a chore. To call Orage's style of writing journalistic would be wrong, but neither is it academic. It does not even lie somewhere in the middle of these, but instead resembles the lost art of the English essayist, perhaps with more in common with a figure like William Hazlitt than the writings of newspaper columnists or scholarly philosophers.

Although Orage's opening gambit might suggest his relationship to Nietzsche's work was one of unalloyed adulation the reality was more complex. It is true Nietzsche struck Orage like a thunderbolt. He was introduced to Nietzsche's work almost accidentally after meeting a textile merchant, George Holbrook Jackson in a Leeds bookshop in 1900.[12] The immediate friendship he and Holbrook Jackson struck up led them to found, with Arthur Penty, the Leeds Arts Club three years later. It has

---

[11] Quoted in James King, *Herbert Read: The Last Modern* (London: Weidenfeld and Nicolson, 1990) p.71

[12] Tom Steele, *Alfred Orage and the Leeds Arts Club* (London: Orage Press, 2009) p.45 and *passim*

the specific aim of 'reducing Leeds to Nietzscheism'.[13]

Notably one of the first meetings of the Leeds Arts Club, chaired by Orage on 7 November 1903, was to discuss Nietzsche, and this was followed by Orage delivering three lectures on Nietzsche at the Arts Club the following February and March. This was at the same arts club that would, barely a decade later, show the first truly abstract paintings to be seen in Britain, works by Wassily Kandinsky.[14] Although Orage was not running the arts club by this date, he was still a significant influence on it, and the connection is not immaterial. Nietzsche was to be as much an influence on eastern European Expressionist artists like Kandinsky as he was on Orage and the Leeds Arts Club.

As this suggests, the Leeds Arts Club was one of the earliest manifestations of a genuinely modernist cultural organisation in Britain. If we define modernism as the shattering of faith in earlier absolute or humanist conceptions of reality then it is easy to see why a modernist organisation like the Leeds Arts Club would be drawn to Nietzsche. The same applies to Orage on a more personal level. In Wallace Martin's estimation the discovery of

---

[13] Luisa Passerini, *Europe in Love, Love in Europe: Imagination and Politics in Britain Between the Wars* (London: IB Tauris, 1998) p.108

[14] Tom Steele, *Alfred Orage and the Leeds Arts Club* (London: Orage Press, 2009) p.190f

Nietzsche enabled Orage to see the limitations of his original philosophical allegiance to Platonism,[15] presumably meaning the limitations inherent in seeking a kind of absolute transcendent truth.

A break with a Platonic conception of truth is certainly apparent here in the chapter 'Beyond Good and Evil' where Orage came very close to using Nietzsche to proffering a form of Existentialist philosophy in which a self-defined reality is the only reality. 'Nietzsche's *Beyond Good and Evil,'* Orage wrote, 'is no more than a criticism of the absolute values of the concepts. He seeks to give to Morality the idea of relativity, which by this time has been given to all other human institutions.' (p.55) But as has been intimated, Orage's understanding of Nietzsche was complex. It is clear from Orage's contemporary interest in the Theosophical Society, and later in the ideas of the Greek mystic George Gurdjieff,[16] that he not ready to give up the search for transcendent truth entirely.

Aside from his continuing interest in spiritualism and mysticism, this potential dissent from Nietzsche manifests itself in two principal ways in Orage's writing. The first is in Orage's tendency to assimilate Nietzsche into a European intellectual

---

[15] Wallace Martin, *Orage as Critic* (London: Routledge, 1974) p.10

[16] K. Paul Johnson, *Initiates of Theosophical Masters* (New York: State University of New York Press, 1995) p.143

framework, rather than seeing him as a categoric break with the humanist tradition. We have already seen this in Orage's comparison between Nietzsche, Goethe and Blake. It is also there in Orage's claim that Nietzsche's concept of the superman, a being that would evolve beyond the human species as it is now known, was not original. According to Orage the superman was in the words of 'every thinker in the past who had projected human virtues upon the magic screen of futurity.' Nonetheless Orage admitted Nietzsche had popularised the notion as never before.[17]

The second dissent is in Orage's tendency to reinterpret Nietzsche to bring him into line with his own thinking. As Wallace Martin suggests it was difficult for Orage to fully embrace the Nietzschean conclusion that all existence is subjective or relative, as later philosophers, including Michel Foucault and Jacques Derrida, were to argue from a starting point in Nietzsche. That threatened to reveal the universe was, in the words of Martin, 'without purpose (and) all action meaningless'.[18] While Orage might have been happy to accept this in relation to morality, particularly as it offered an antidote to the stultifying morality of provincial and still essentially Victorian

---

[17] Tom Steele, *Alfred Orage and the Leeds Arts Club* (London: Orage Press, 2009) p.72

[18] Wallace Martin, *Orage as Critic* (London: Routledge, 1974) p.15

Britain, he was less inclined to accept it as a general rule, and so he bends Nietzsche's philosophy to accommodate this disinclination. Thus Orage's search for esoteric truths finds a clear outlet in *Friedrich Nietzsche: The Dionysian Spirit of the Age* when Orage claims Nietzsche's philosophy is itself essentially mystical, whilst admitting Nietzsche would not be happy to hear it described that way. (p. 57).

As a consequence we see Orage define the superman not simply as a new evolved being, but as a kind of enlightened figure, almost Buddha like in its relationship to the unenlightened mass of humanity. We have of course to be careful in over stressing this aspect of Orage's book, as Orage was at pains to point out that the superman is not so beyond material being he would cease to be physical. 'Whatever the superman may be psychologically,' wrote Orage, 'there is no doubt that physically he must be capable of living on the earth.' (p.52) Nonetheless the mystical strand in Orage's thinking is there.

As we can see Orage is careful not to delineate the coming superman too much. In the final chapter Orage discusses what the race of supermen might be like. They will not be like the coming philosophers, he tells us, whose role seems to be to act much as John the Baptist was as the forerunner to the coming of Christ. Nor will the supermen be like us.

Whatever we are, Orage effectively says, the supermen are not. Instead the superman is as different from a man as a man is from a tiger, and so, Orage insists, just as one cannot say a man 'is a tiger writ large' we cannot assume a superman is a man writ large. (p.51). The superman is something different, something that even Nietzsche could not imagine or envisage. All Nietzsche could do, Orage claims, was tell us what the superman will not be: it is not us, and it is not even the best of us.

In this we have perhaps the first sign of the enduring legacy of Orage's book. Orage reconfigured Nietzsche's materialism by fusing it with an immaterial transcendentalism drawn from his own investigations into spiritualism, mysticism and even early psychoanalysis. He was not alone in doing so with similar reinterpretations of Nietzsche elsewhere in Europe at the time, particularly amongst German and eastern European Expressionist artists and writers. Indeed it is probably best to see Orage in the context of European Expressionist thinking in the way he recasts Nietzsche.

Like many of the European Expressionists Orage seems unwilling to let go of the notion of an esoteric reality existing beyond the human perceptions of normal reality. Like them some residual Platonist thinking seems to remain in Orage so that there is a continuing dualism between the normal and ordinary one one side, and the esoteric and extraordinary on the other. This becomes apparent in *Friedrich Nietzsche: The Dionysian Spirit of the Age* when Orage makes an extraordinary claim for the Christian Church, that its leaders should have been those who worked actively to bring the race of supermen into being. They should have led us from the normal and ordinary life of being human to the esoteric and extraordinary life of being superhuman he claims. The failure of the Church to do this lies in its obsession with Heaven and the afterlife. As a result, Orage tells us, the only 'race it has sought to create is an other-worldly race.' (p.52).

What this suggests is that Orage conceives of Nietzsche as a philosopher who hypothesises two states of existence, the known world of now (normal, ordinary and human) and the unknown possibility of the future (esoteric, extraordinary and superhuman). It took a slightly younger generation, including most notably Herbert Read, to take Orage's conception of Nietzsche and recognise that this hypothesis was itself an Apollonian and Dionysian divide, between the normal, ordinary and human reality of Apollo and the esoteric, extraordinary and superhuman reality of Dionysos. It is hard not to link this, as it undoubtedly must have been in Orage's mind, to the Dionysian (or Orphic) Mysteries of the ancient

Greek world, which promised access to esoteric knowledge through secret sacred rituals.[19]

The importance of this dualism, or dialectic, should not be underestimated. Read was the key figure in the dissemination of modernist thinking in the English speaking world and beyond.[20] But it was very much a modernism underpinned by Orage's conception of Nietzsche that Read promoted. This can be seen in one example from Read's extensive output. Co-opting a phrase coined by the sculptor Eric Gill, 'to hell with culture', Read makes a highly significant distinction between culture and art.[21] That division is in simple terms the same as the one Orage sees in Nietzsche, between the normal, ordinary and human reality of Apollo and the esoteric, extraordinary and superhuman reality of Dionysos. (p.35) The only distinction is the names Apollo and Dionysos are expunged. Apollo is effectively the known reality of culture and Dionysos the unknown reality of art. And just as Orage's

---

[19] Notably this was discussed at the time, particularly in relation to the similarities between Dionysian and Christian esoteric knowledge, as in Paul Carus, 'The Greek Mysteries: A Preparation for Christianity', in *The Monist*, vol.11, no.1, October, 1900.

[20] See Michael Paraskos, 'The Curse of King Bomba' in Michael Paraskos (ed.) *Re-Reading Read: New Views on Herbert Read* (London: Freedom Press, 2007) p.44f

[21] Herbert Read, 'To Hell with Culture', in Herbert Read, *To Hell with Culture* (London: Routledge, 1963)

Nietzsche saw the struggle in Greek culture as being between the Dionysian and Apollonian, so Read comes to argue that the struggle of art is against culture. Art is in effect the cry of *to hell with culture.*

We are always right in this context to talk about Orage's Nietzsche rather than simply Nietzsche. It was specifically Orage's Nietzsche that Herbert Read took on board, and in doing so Read also took on some of Orage's uncertainty about full blown Nietzscheanism. This is even apparent in the relative value of the Apollonian and Dionysian. While it might seem as though Orage, like Nietzsche, prioritised Dionysos this is not quite the case with either Orage or Read. In hypothesising the two opposite tendencies of the Apollonian and Dionysian, Nietzsche did not appear to consider Apollo and Dionysos of equal worth. Certainly the reputation of Nietzsche amongst most of his supporters and detractors was that Dionysos was prioritised as the vital element in life, while Apollo seemed to stultify that vitality. Even in Nietzsche's work the relationship between Apollo and Dionysos is ambiguous as Nietzsche's preference for Dionysos sits alongside a recognition that both Dionysos and Apollo are necessary. At best it can be described as a matter of preference for Dionysos on Nietzsche's part, rather than a balancing act in accepting them both. But in Orage's commentary a balance of the two was more definitely asserted. Orage wrote:

> Apollo and Dionysos may stand respectively for law and liberty, duty and love, custom and change, science and intuition, art and inspiration: in their larger aspects they are symbols of oppositions that penetrate the very stuff of consciousness and life; they are its warp and woof. Thus Apollo stands for Form as against Dionysos for Life; for matter as against Energy; for the Human as against the Superhuman. Apollo is always on the side of the formed, the definite, the restrained, the rational; but Dionysos is the power that destroys forms, that leads the definite into the infinite, the unrestrained, the tumultuous and passionate.

What this means is that although Nietzsche wrote of reconciliation of these unequal forces in *The Birth of Tragedy*, it is in Orage that we see a far clearer suggestion that neither Dionysos nor Apollo are preeminent. 'Dionysos without Apollo would be unmanifest, pure energy', Orage wrote. 'Apollo without Dionysos would de dead, inert.' (p.33-4)

The premise of balanced forces was to become a key element in Read's art and literary theory from the 1930s through to the 1960s.[22] Out of this Read

---

[22] See David Thistlewood, *Herbert Read Formlessness and Form* (London: Routledge, 1984) p. 30; and Tom Steele, *Alfred Orage and the Leeds Arts Club* (London: Orage Press, 2009). p.186.

came to see a correlation with other dialectical systems being discussed at the time, ranging from the historic dichotomy between classicism and romanticism, to the division of introverted and extroverted character types in psychoanalysis, and the artistic division between Constructivism and Surrealism. In each case it was Orage's balancing out of the Apollonian against the Dionysian that underpinned Read's approach, not a prioritisation given to Dionysos. As Read noted Nietzsche's Dionysos 'is conceived as a blind will, a fever, a frenzy, and is too negative for our own philosophy of art'. What was needed instead was a dialectic of equal opposites from which one could achieve a balanced synthesis.[23]

This is apparent even in Read's division between Apollonian culture and Dionysian art, for although Read might have used the bombastic statement *to hell with culture,* this was in a context of post-Second World War thinking that was increasingly seeing art and culture as the same thing. A little bombast was needed to try to redress this imbalance, but for the most part Read conceived of the culture and art relationship as a self-balancing process, art being formed at the cusp of the unknown future and then being transformed into culture in the known present and past. This pattern

---

[23] Herbert Read, *Icon and Idea* (London: Faber, 1955) p. 51.

fits in readily with Orage's Nietzsche. (p.38) In this way Read formulated a dialectical understanding of art in which the greatest art is not to be found at either the Apollonian or Dionysian ends of the cultural spectrum, but in their balanced unity, something which he believed was evident in artists such as Henry Moore and Pablo Picasso.

With his open hostility to Read the American art critic Clement Greenberg was never likely to admit his own conception of Nietzsche's balanced Apollo and Dionysos was derived from Read, but the typological similarities provide compelling circumstantial evidence that Read was his source.[24] What is of significance in the context of this reissue of Orage's book, however, is that Read derived his understanding of this theory initially from Orage, and more specifically, from Orage's *Friedrich Nietzsche: The Dionysian Spirit of the Age.* From there, whether one followed Read or Greenberg, it became one of the mainstream defining factors of modernism.

---

[24] A key text here is Clement Greenberg's essay 'The Present Prospects for American Painting and Sculpture', in *Horizon,* October 1947, reproduced in Clement Greenberg, *The Collected Essays and Criticism, Volume 2: Arrogant Purpose, 1945-1949* (Chicago: University of Chicago Press, 1988) p.160f. Greenberg goes out of his way to mock British art in this essay, and by implication the chief apologist of those artists Herbert Read. This implies that Greenberg is trying to hide his own Readian footprints. For additional comment see Marcia Brennan 'The Multiple Masculinities of Canonical Modernism: James Johnson Sweeney and Alfred H. Barr Jr. in the 1930s' in Anna Brzyski (ed.) *Partisan Canons* (Durham: Duke University Press, 2007) p. 200, n.35.

Alfred Orage

Nietzsche

The Dionysian Spirit of the Age

CHAPTER ONE
His Life

Friedrich Nietzsche is the greatest European event since Goethe. From one end of Europe to the other, wherever his books are read, the discussion in the most intellectual and aristocratically minded circles turns on the problems raised by him. In Germany and in France his name is the war cry of opposing factions, and before very long his name will be familiar in England. Already half a dozen well-known English writers might be named who owe, if not half their ideas, at least half the courage of their ideas to Nietzsche. Ibsen seems almost mild by the side of him.

Emerson, with whom he had much in common, seems strangely cool: William Blake alone among English writers seems to have closely resembled Nietzsche, and he who has read the *Marriage of Heaven and Hell*, and grasped its significance, will have little to learn from the apostle of Zarathustra. In other respects, however, Nietzsche is incomparably more encyclopaedic than Blake or Emerson or lbsen. He stood near the pinnacle of European culture, a scholar among scholars and a thinker among thinkers. His range of subjects is as wide as modern thought. Nobody is more representative of the spirit of the age. In sum, he was his age; he comprehended the mind of Europe.

It is all the more significant therefore that Nietzsche's main attack should be levelled against the foundations of European morality. Yet nothing less bold and titanic was his declared task and mission. The greatest immoralist the modern world has seen, he needed the qualities he possessed in order to stand alone against a continent and the tradition of two thousand years. Passion was indeed the characteristic of his thought; of the proverbial calm of the philosopher he had none. Great problems, he said, demanded great love: and in his search for problems and solutions he was more a devouring fire than a dry light. There has been nobody more moving in literature.

There are books that appeal to sentiment, books that appeal to the mind, and books that appeal to the will. Nietzsche's belong to this last small but immortal section. Nobody can read his books without receiving a powerful stimulus in one direction or another. There is something strangely significant of his own life in the title of his first book: *The Birth of Tragedy.* Wagner he named a stage player of the spirit; but Nietzsche was the tragedian in the spiritual drama of Mansoul. His very style is tragical and heavy with the rustle of prophet's robes. His voice now rises to a loud exultant shout, and now drops to the sibilant hiss of the arch conspirator. But there is no trace of bombast, the overblowing wind of little ideas with the wind of big words; his matter is quite as tragical and moving as his manner.

There is nothing diffuse or turgid in his style; whoever expects to find Carlylean rhetoric will be disappointed. Out of the oppressive thunder-cloud of his thought come shooting at every moment splendidly bright aphorisms like forked lightning; they are his thunderbolts carefully forged and shaped and sharpened. It is as an aphorist that he will live in literature even should an emancipated Europe forget her moral warriors. Heine may be remembered as he wished to be remembered, for the brave soldier he was in the war of the liberation of humanity. Ibsen is the splendid divisional general. But Nietzsche is in command of the whole of the iron artillery. Like them he knows his enemy; even better than they he knows where the enemy is weakest.

Of the outward life of this strange incarnation of European unrest there is little to record. The greatest events, he says somewhere, are the greatest thoughts, the product of our stillest hours.

He was born in 1844 at Rocken near Lutzen in Saxony, and was of Polish descent on his father's side. This latter fact gave him a pardonable pride, for he remembered that the Pole Copernicus had reversed the judgment of a world; that the Pole Chopin had challenged German music; why should not the Pole Nietzsche reverse the judgment of his world? In 1845, when Fritz was only a year old, his father died from the effects of a fall. The family was taken to Naumburg, where, later on, Fritz was sent to the village school. As a boy, his sister tells us, he was very pious: and he seems to have had the rare desire to put his piety into practice. This was always characteristic of Nietzsche. 'We Nietzsches,' said one of his aunts, 'hate lies': and lies for Nietzsche always meant cowardice, and cowardice meant no more than the shirking of practising one's belief.

We hear but little of him during the years 1845-58: –a little dabbling in poetry, a good deal of serious work in music, a continual meditation on the problems to which later his life was to be given. In 1858 he was sent to a school at Pforta, and there in the following year he came into contact with the greatest emotional force of Germany at that day, Wagnerian music. He heard the magical music of *Tristan and Isolde.* That was the first real event of his life, the event that moved his soul to its depths. Henceforward he was a Wagnarian.

But the passion thus stirred he turned into the channels of his ethical thought. Though aesthetically moved he was not content to remain in the sterile region of pure aesthetics. His whole passion, says his sister, still lay in the world of knowledge, where it had now become a raging fire. In 1865 he entered as a student at Leipsic University, where he began his career as a professed student of classical philology.

But a more important event than classical philology befell him there –he read Schopenhauer. Only one whose fortune brings him, after years of arid solitary thought, suddenly and as if by chance, into a world of thought and of men such as he has dreamed of but never realized, can understand Nietzsche's emotion on first reading Schopenhauer. Keats thus met Homer, and his wonderful sonnet is the record. Nietzsche's record is an exultation in impassioned prose. He felt, he said, as if every word in Schopenhauer was addressed directly and solely to him. There for the first time his eyes dwelt upon the sunlit region of art, upon a mind and a world such as he had dimly conceived and greatly dreamed. If in later life he threw aside one by one all the doctrines of Schopenhauer, it was as a David might put away the weapons of Saul –only because he had proved them.

In 1868 he met Wagner in person, and the two became fast friends till the fatal year 1876, when with an enormous effort Nietzsche began to break away from the master, who, he thought, had played the renegade. From 1869 to 1880 he held the Chair of Classical Philology at Basel. In 1872 his first book was published –*The Birth of Tragedy.* It was dedicated to Wagner, and is the acknowledgment of Nietzsche's debt to art.

But already he began to see the new world, his own world, opening before him. His next books were a series of notes on moral origins, in which we see him digging about the foundations of men's good and evil, cautiously, carefully, but unflinchingly. In 1876, from his break with Wagner, he began deliberately to place himself at the head of the moral reformation of Europe. Whatever personal considerations may have entered as excuses, his quarrel with Wagner was inevitable from the publication of Wagner's *Parsifal.* Of that work Nietzsche could scarcely speak with toleration. It was for him the death-knell of his hopes, and henceforth Wagner was the head and front of his abomination.

By 1880 Nietzsche's health had so declined that he was compelled to resign his Chair at Basel. Nine years he spent in traveling in Italy and Switzerland, where he meditated and wrote his later books. In 1885 his *Zarathustra* was published. This marks the final period of Nietzsche's productive life. It was the period of the Superman. From the time the idea of a splendid type of humanity came to him as the redeeming creation of a world of all too human men, Nietzsche believed and ever grew in the belief that his mission was to preach Superman. Already in 1876 his friends had observed that he placed an extraordinary importance on his work; but from the birth of Zarathustra Nietzsche conceived the idea that he was no less than the avatara of the spirit of humanity. In a brilliant essay he describes the consciousness such as the genius of humanity may be supposed to enjoy, the complete and ever present knowledge, memory and rich experience, of all ages and times, the visions and plans of all the future. And wild as the notion may seem, there is little doubt that Nietzsche had risen to something like this height.

In 1889 the final blow came which shattered the lamp of Nietzsche and threw in the dust the brightest intellectual light that Europe knew. A period of severe hallucinatory delirium led on to complete dementia: the enormous strain of thought sustained at white heat during a period of thirty years broke down at last a brain which after all was human and fragile. Nietzsche passed out of sight of men, and died a few months later without recovering sanity.

CHAPTER TWO
Apollo or Dionysos?

Whoever wishes to understand Greek culture, said Nietzsche, must first penetrate the mystery of Dionysos. The statement is equally true if we substitute for Greek culture Nietzsche himself. The secret of Nietzsche is the secret of Dionysos. It was through the gateway of Greek tragic art that Nietzsche found his way into his own world: and all his originality and daring, as well as his excesses and contradictions, become intelligible when once his tragic view is seized.

In his study of Greek art, Nietzsche was struck by a fact which had puzzled many thinkers before him. Why did the Greeks, the blithest and best constituted race the world has ever seen, need such a tragic art as theirs? For they were not emotionally asleep, nor was it as a medicinal purgation of soul that they suffered tragedy. On the contrary, they were a highly impressionable, profoundly aesthetic people, and the evidence shows them deeply moved, yet greatly rejoicing, in the tragic drama. Yet what need had they of tragedy?

It is plain from the form of the question that Nietzsche's conception of art was not the ordinary conception. The art of a people was not to be accounted for by their whims and fancies; it was to be determined by need. What does not spring from necessity is not art. Unless a people need art as they need bread, how can their art be great? But to satisfy what imperious need did the Greeks create tragedy?

Nietzsche found the solution of the problem in the myth of Apollo and Dionysos: and the antithesis he there discovered he afterwards employed in art, literature, philosophy, morality, and life itself. Mythology, he saw, was no less than the spiritual history of a people, the records of its moods, its periods of spiritual doubt, despair, and triumph. In the story of the coming of Dionysos into Greece, of the resistance of Apollo, and of the final reconciliation, Nietzsche saw the outlines of spiritual movements mythically veiled, the phases of the myth corresponding to historic phases of the Greek mind.

The coming of Dionysos was a popular movement of ideas: the resistance of Apollo was a popular movement of conservatism: the reconciliation was a compromise. Regarded in this way, the myth becomes history of the most intimate nature, and records the history of the Greek soul during several centuries.

All the more interesting is the story to us on account of the essential similarity between ancient Greece and modern Europe. The issues involved in the struggle of Apollo and Dionysos are the same now as then. In truth, as Nietzsche discovered, the way to the modern world is through the portals of the ancient wisdom. The spiritual condition of Greece during the period immediately preceding the Dionysian awakening was comparable to the spiritual condition of Europe during the eighteenth century. Greece was Apollan* in the sense that Europe was religious. The long established Apollan cult was fast becoming a convention. Now that the Titans, the elemental forces of wild nature, were vanquished, and the Gods had no more enemies, Olympos, the bright and splendid Olympos, began visibly to fade. Great Zeus himself was nodding on his throne. Religion, morality, art, life itself, were losing their hold on men, and Greece was threatened with the fate of India.

Then it was that there came into Greece from the north, the home of spiritual impulse, a new power in the form of Dionysos. That its leader was a Thracian, that he brought with him the secret of wine, music, and ecstasy, that he was instantly welcomed by women, and that the movement so inaugurated began rapidly to spread over Greece –all this is clear enough even in the secular story. But the spiritual issues were infinitely greater. For Dionysos and the Dionysian spirit were everywhere in open and direct antagonism with everything Apollan. The whole structure of the Greek mind

**Apollonian*

under Apollan influence was threatened at every point by the attacks of the Dionysians. Its modes of thought, its religion, its morality, its art, its philosophy, its very existence, were challenged. In comparison with all that Greece had so far been, the Dionysian movement was revolutionary, irreligious, immoral, barbaric, and anarchic.

The reception of such a movement by the Apollan Greeks may easily be conceived by modern Europeans. However they might secretly feel the attraction of the splendid virility of the new movement, they could not but pause before accepting doctrines which flew in the face of accepted established customs. It was true that the established customs were stale, that Olympos was fading, that Greece was dying; but the admission of Dionysos, with his train of ecstatic women, wild men, and still wilder doctrines, seemed a remedy worse than the disease.

Placed once more in a position of necessity, Apollo girded himself for the fight: and the conservative forces for a while succeeded in repelling the Dionysian invaders. Thus, by a curious reaction, the very element that threatened to destroy, served in fact to strengthen and renew.

But such an effect did not pass unnoticed among the Greeks. It would be absurd to suppose that many individual Greeks were clearly aware of the problems they were facing. Spiritual movements are conscious in the minds of only a few, but they have their home in the mind of the race.

The question that now presented itself was this: remembering Olympos at war with Titans, Olympos at rest and dying of rest, and Olympos renewing its youth in war with Dionysos, was it possible, was it really true, that Olympos needed an enemy, that conflict was indispensable to Olympus?

Sworn deadly enemy of Apollo as Dionysos might be, could Apollo really live without him? Might not Dionysos, the eternal foe, be also the eternal saviour of Apollo? The question was afterwards put by Nietzsche in myriads of forms. The whole of his work may be said, indeed, to be no less than the raising of this terrible interrogation mark. He divined and stated the problem for modern Europe as it had been stated for ancient Greece. He asked Europe the question which Greece had already asked herself, and which Greece had magnificently answered. For the answer of Greece is recorded in her Tragic Mysteries. In Greek tragic drama the answer of the Greek mind to the momentous question is a splendid affirmative. Not Apollo alone; not Dionysos alone; but Apollo and Dionysos.

What will be Europe's reply? Before, however, considering any further the meaning of Greek tragedy, it is advisable to glance briefly at the issues involved in the eternal antagonism. While, in their human aspects, Apollo and Dionysos may stand respectively for law and liberty, duty and love, custom and change, science and intuition,art and inspiration: in their larger aspects they are symbols of oppositions that penetrate the very stuff of consciousness and life; they are its warp and woof. Thus Apollo stands for Form as against Dionysos for Life; for Matter as against Energy; for the Human as against the Superhuman. Apollo is always on the side of the formed, the definite, the restrained, the rational; but Dionysos is the power that destroys forms, that leads the definite into the infinite, the unrestrained, the tumultuous and passionate. In perhaps their profoundest antithesis, Dionysos is pure energy (which Blake, a thorough Dionysian, said was eternal delight) while Apollo is pure form, seeking ever to veil and blind pure energy.

Life, as it thus appears to the eye of the imaginative mind, is the spectacle of the eternal play and conflict of two mutually opposing principles: Dionysos ever escaping from the forms that Apollo is ever creating for him. And it is just this unceasing conflict that is the essence of life itself; life is conflict. Dionysos without Apollo would be unmanifest, pure energy. Apollo without Dionysos would be dead, inert. Each is necessary to the other, but in active opposition: for, as stage by stage the play proceeds, Apollo must build continually more beautiful, more enduring forms, which Dionysos, in turn, must continually surmount and transcend. The drama of life is thus a perpetual movement towards a climax that never comes. Apollo never will imprison Dionysos forever: Dionysos never will escape forever from Apollo. Only, as in the early stages of life, Dionysos begins by speaking in the language of Apollo; Apollo will, in the later phases, learn more and more to speak in the language of Dionysos. Life itself will become Dionysian as the eternal conflict proceeds.

In the Greek drama, Nietzsche, as has been said, found at once the problem and its solution. For what could life have meant to the spectators of the plays of Aeschylus and Sophocles? What but the tragedy of the eternal strife, the recognition of the essential tragedy of life itself, the spectacle of a never ending world-drama in which the gods played? For the tragic Greeks, life was the Dionysian will-to-renew, at war with the Apollan will-to-preserve; life was intelligible only as an aesthetic spectacle; there was no finality, no purpose, no end, no goal; only the gods played ceaselessly. And the business of man was to assist at the spectacle and in the play. As a joyous spectator-actor he should enter into the strife, consciously aiding the unfolding of the eternal drama, of which he himself was both Dionysos and Apollo. For, as the world-drama is in truth the drama of mind, so the interior nature of the individual is the stage on which it is played.

The perception of this truth by the Greeks was the signal of the reconciliation of Apollo and Dionysos. As at Delphi, the home of Apollo, the priests of Dionysos were formally admitted with their train of ceremony and festival; so in the life of the race and in the minds of the Greeks themselves the reconciliation took place. Henceforth, Greek culture was the child of both Dionysos and Apollo. And in the Tragic Mysteries was revealed to the spectator an image of the life of the world. On the stage he beheld Dionysos and the Dionysified struggling against the Apollan powers of Fate and Death.

The Greek needed to behold that struggle. He needed to be constantly reassured that life was of this nature. Profoundly as he might and must sympathise with the sufferings of Apollo, he could not but sympathise even more deeply with the agonies of Dionysos. Yet in the end he could not be mortally distressed. For he felt that, fierce and terrible as the conflict was, real and moving as the pains of the tragedy must needs be, it was the game, the play, the celestial life of gods that he was witnessing. To rise to the height where he might joyfully behold the game without ceasing for an instant to feel the pain and sorrow of it all; to rejoice with Dionysos victorious, and yet to mourn with Apollo slain; to assist in his own life the great drama by welcoming all that promised struggle; finally, to will with all his soul the increasing triumph of Dionysos, that life and joy might be all in all –such was the meaning of Tragedy among the Greeks.

When Nietzsche had reached this conclusion, he turned to the closer examination of his own Europe. In the music of *Tristan and Isolde* he heard, or thought he heard, the old Dionysian strains. He believed that Europe was about to enter, through Wagner, into a repetition of the spiritual history of the Greeks. Dionysos, he thought, had come to Europe. And if the events in Greece were to be repeated in Europe,we were already on the threshold of the new era. With Dionysos at our gates, and the spirit of joy, freedom, excess; the spirit of pure energy, the old cry of life desiring to renew itself –how could a chosen disciple of Dionysos be silent? Nietzsche threw himself into the struggle, even as he believed Dionysos, the spirit of life itself, had already done. For was not Dionysos:

> ...The spirit of the years to come,
> Yearning to mix himself with life?

Later, he regretted having mistaken Wagner for a genuine Dionysian, and reflected that the Dionysian swans of his enthusiasm were no more than geese. But he never doubted that the history of the Greeks was about to be repeated. Failing Wagner, he himself would be the Dionysian initiator. He would transform Europe, and deliver men's minds from the dull oppression of Apollo. He began from that time the enormous labour of turning the Dionysian criticism on the whole fabric of European civilisation.

If he is so largely negative in his effects the cause is not to be sought so much in him as in the times. Positive doctrines he had in abundance. Later in life he deplored the negations into which he had been led. But the work of undermining the foundations of modern thought occupied too large a part of a comparatively brief life.

Hence we see in his work more of the struggle and less of the triumph of Dionysos. Even in this it is Greek history repeated, for Dionysos also was defeated at first.

CHAPTER THREE
Beyond Good and Evil

When Nietzsche found himself on the other side of Dionysos he found himself on the other side likewise of Good and Evil. These terms, as ordinarily employed, ceased to have any value for him; but their meaning was greater.

His book, under the strange title *Beyond Good and Evil*, was at once a challenge and an attack on morality. Such an attack cannot fail at first sight to appear wild and criminal in the extreme. And Nietzsche was thoroughly well aware of this. It is quite unnecessary to plead any extenuation, or to make it appear that Nietzsche was playing a part. Nobody was ever more serious; he set his whole mind on the task of destroying morality, root and branch.

He challenged not merely this or that item of the current code, he desired to annihilate the very conception of the code. He was not merely immoral, he aimed at being unmoral, super-moral. Morality was to be completely transcended.

In the space of this chapter it will be impossible to outline more than a few of the leading ideas of Nietzsche's theory. And first, what is the nature of the morality against which he thunders and lightens?

It is no easy matter to define Morality, and Nietzsche himself made more than one unsuccessful attempt. The two essential elements, however, of any system of morality are, first, the scheduling of certain actions, thoughts and desires as Good, and of others as Evil; and secondly, the addition of a religious sanction, whereby good actions become stamped with divine approval, and bad actions with divine disapproval.

Against these two elements Nietzsche therefore directed his critical guns. Regarding the first element, the classification of actions into good and evil, Nietzsche's line of attack was to show what may be called the natural history of such classifications. Every nation, every individual, every organism, must by its very nature make a choice among things. An individual, in fact, is constituted and defined by its selective power. But it does not at all follow, because an individual or nation must choose and select that the choice and selection are advantageous to it. Over and over again we have seen individuals choosing and selecting not what is good for them, but what is bad for them. Compelled to judge, they are by no means compelled to judge rightly: and since nations and peoples are no less fallible than individuals, it follows that the value of every code of morality which embodies a people's judgments is to be judged by another standard than the code itself.

The interrogations which Nietzsche places against every code of morality are in essence these: Is this morality conducive to the ends proposed? Is this people mistaken in its judgments? Are its good and its evil really good and evil for its spiritual welfare? But the answer to the question depends upon another question –the value of the people whose judgment is being considered.

We ordinarily discount the value of the judgment of inexperienced persons. The judgments of the young and the old, for example, are often diametrically opposed. The judgments of a people as old as the Chinese are very different from the judgments of, say, the modern Americans. In considering the value of a moral code we have, therefore, to inquire into the value of the people which created it. How came they to invent just such a code? *Why* did they name this action good, and that bad? Again, were they mistaken ?

In approaching this problem Nietzsche makes use of a capital distinction. All life, he says, is either ascendant or decadent. Every organism, whether an individual, a people, or a race, belongs either to an ascending or a descending current. And its morality, art, form of society, instincts, and in fact its whole mode of manifestation, depend on whether it belongs to one or the other order of being. The primary characteristic of the ascending life is the consciousness of inexhaustible power. The individual or people behind which the flowing tide of life-force moves is creative, generous, reckless, enthusiastic, prodigal, passionate: its virtues, be it observed, are Dionysian. Its will-to-power is vigorous; in energy it finds delight. And the moral code of such a people will reflect faithfully the people's power.

But the primary characteristic of the descending life is the consciousness of *declining* power. The individual or people in whom the life-force is ebbing instinctively husband their resources. They are preservative rather than creative, niggardly, careful, fearful of passion and excess, calculating and moderate. And, in turn, their code of morality faithfully reflects their Will.

Looking thus upon any morality as no more than a symptom of the physiological condition of a race, the question of good and evil is in reality irrelevant. No symptom, as such, can be either good or bad. A morality expresses the judgments of a people, its diagnosis of its own health, its self-decreed regimen. And as such it may be-mistaken!

But Nietzsche discovered another division in moralities. According as the code of morality current among a people originated in the aristocracy or in the mob, he named the morality Noble-morality, or Slave-morality. Doubtless, in aristocratic communities such as those in Europe, the disparity between the moral codes of the aristocracy and the democracy is very great, amounting in many respects to simple contrast. But, as Nietzsche himself says, even the most aristocratic communities are not aristocratic in the real sense. 'Mob at the top, mob below,' is his description of Europe. Thus, his aristocratic or noble-morality must not be equated with the morality of noblemen and the wealthy classes, nor his slave-morality with that of the democracy. If the division is of any value it must be applied to the personality, and not to possessions or position.

In this sense there is a world of difference between the code of morality of the noble-minded man and the code of the mean and the petty-minded. Nietzsche carries the distinction into the furthest fields. Noble-morality, he says, is classic morality, the morality of Greece, of Rome,of Renaissance Italy, of ancient India. But Christian morality is slave-morality *in excelsis*. For the essence of Christian morality is the desire of the individual to be saved; his consciousness of power is so small that he lives in hourly peril of damnation and death, and yearns thus for the arms of some saving grace. The Christian, in fact, seeks a master, as all slaves must: and en lieu of a real master, he will invent for himself imaginary masters. But the essence of noble-morality is the desire to command, the will to be master, the idea of freedom, the sense of power, gratitude towards life, and the realisation of the privileges of responsibility.

Of any code of morality, therefore, Nietzsche has this further question to ask: In what class of mind did it originate? Whose valuation of things does it express, the valuation of the noble mind or of the slave mind? It will be seen that these and the questions before named go to the roots of the problem of Morality.

Every people has thought that its morality was right, that its Good was good forever, its Evil evil forever. But the comparative study of moralities begun by Nietzsche already begins to demonstrate the fact that there is in reality no absolute Good, no absolute Evil. Of nothing is it any longer possible to say : This is Good everywhere and always; that is Bad everywhere and always. Good and Bad must be determined on every occasion afresh, and always in relation to a definite purpose, by which alone anything can be either good or bad. *'Only he who knoweth whither he saileth knoweth which is his fair wind and which is his foul wind.'*

Thus in one sense Nietzsche's *Beyond Good and Evil* is no more than a criticism of the absolute values of these concepts. He seeks to give to Morality the idea of relativity, which by this time has been given to all other human institutions: not Good and Evil as if things were these absolutely, but Good and Bad in relation to a definitely conceived end.

But, as we have seen, the absolute idea is well-nigh essential to Morality. How can unquestioning obedience be claimed for laws which themselves are open to question? And this authority is given by the association of morality with religion, or rather with theology. On theology, therefore, Nietzsche levels his second attack.

Every dominant code of morality has naturally endeavoured to secure the support of every power in the state. *'All instincts aspire to tyranny.'* Not only are the secular powers of legal punishment ranged on the side of a popular morality, but the theological powers as well. From whatever class the code of morality has issued, and to whatever type of life the community has belonged, the code has been declared divine as well as human. This has produced some strange inconsistencies, as when the same God is appealed to on behalf of both parties to a war. But the essential fact is that a code of action,in order to become a morality at all, must have religious sanction. Destroy the religious sanction, and the moral code falls to the level of taste and expediency. It becomes a rational institution, of no more significance and of no more authority than the ordinary law of the land, or than the rules of etiquette. It is, in fact, by the assistance of the religious sanction that a code of manners becomes a code of morality.

Now Nietzsche is far from denying the right of a community to add the terrors of theology to the terrors of the law on behalf of its code. But the value of the code is thereby not increased; nor do human laws which win a theological sanction become necessarily infallible. As a matter of fact, there are examples in history of codes of morality sanctioned by the prevailing theology which proved ruinous to the community. May it not be that our code of morality, sanctioned as it is by our theology, will prove ruinous to us?

In any case the support of theology is paid for dearly. Suppose that every Act of Parliament were declared to be the Will of God, and that men believed them to be the Will of God, (*'belief and fact are by no means synonymous,'*) such Acts would continue to be, as they are, fallible and imperfect. Of that there is no doubt. But the very belief in their infallibility and sanctity would paralyse men's efforts to alter and improve them.

Instead of the sensible recognition that institutions and ordinances of men are in their very nature temporary and expedient, We should have in the sphere of Parliamentary laws the intolerable dogma of the eternal nature of human law.
But this is exactly the price paid for the elevation of manners into morality by means of theology.

Theology universalises. When once a human law has taken to itself a divine sanction, it ceases to be capable of regarding itself as temporary, fallible, particular in its application, questionable –in short, human! Morality ceases to be human, and becomes divine –and inhuman. The proper and necessary classification which society must make of good things and bad things, of things to be allowed and of things to be forbidden, of things to be praised and of things to be condemned,–this sensible and necessary classification of things according to a purpose which society has in mind becomes the very instrument of society's destruction just so soon as these tentative, partial, and experimental classifications become universalised, theologised, and petrified. Thereafter it is difficult even for society itself to revise its judgments. Every philosopher who lays hands on the moral code becomes by the act itself both a criminal and an impious heretic.

The noblest service a man can render his generation, namely, to exchange its false goods for real goods, becomes a service that he can render only at peril to his life. By morality sin came into the world; for the price of morality is sin and crime.

A parallel effect of theology on manners is to raise to the position of absolute power the particular valuation which has chanced to become relatively dominant. It has already been said that the theological sanction has at different times been accorded to the most opposite codes of morality. In Europe, according to Nietzsche, the code of manners which secured theological sanction issued from the slave caste. As morality, however, it becomes universal; and as universal, it fits only those who are temperamentally similar to the founders of the code. As these are in a small minority, the universalising of the code forces on the majority in the community a system which is either too great or too small for them. It is thus most certainly true that conformity to the moral code, while difficult, nay, impossible to many, is easy, and fatally easy, to others.

Thus in some it produces hypocrisy, cant, humbug, and other symptoms of an over-heavy burden of responsibility ; and in others, deadly indifference, *ennui,* and pessimism. For it is asking too much of vulgar natures that they shall act as noble natures : and it is asking too little of noble natures that they shall act as vulgar natures. Yet no less than this universalism is implied and involved in the elevation of a Good and Bad into a universal Good and Evil.

Nietzsche has much more to say, but here we are following the main lines only. His final conclusion is, as we have seen, the need to transcend Morality; in other words, to dismiss from our minds the conceptions of Good and Evil as absolute things, and to substitute for them the human valuations Good and Bad. With the theological concepts of Good and Evil would go also the theological machinery of those concepts, the idea of Sin, or the need for Salvation, the idea of divine punishment, the bad conscience, the sense of guilt, remorse... all the degenerate instincts, the negative instincts.

What would take their place would be the sense of responsibility, or rather the privilege of responsibility, and the will to create for the future, unhindered by the dead hand of the past.

But the questions: Good for What? Bad for what? remain as yet unanswered. When we have abolished Good and Evil, ceased to believe in a divine will, and declared that man alone and his purposes are writ in the world –what then? Has man any goal by which he may judge of things whether they are Good or Bad?

No measurement is possible without a standard. Man *must* measure, but by what shall he measure? Shall he measure all things by their power to produce happiness? We shall see in the next chapter Nietzsche's standard. It is his positive doctrine, the crown and the justification of all his criticism and destruction. His goal is The Superman.

CHAPTER FOUR
The Superman

There are two possible ends towards which to make progress consciously: the earthly end, and what Nietzsche has called the otherworldly end. In the absence of any positive knowledge of the nature or even the existence of any future life, it is folly, Nietzsche declared, to train a race by morality, religion, and all the other instruments of education for a future of which we can know nothing. For what we do know, we may, however, make ourselves responsible. And the certain thing is, that humanity lives, has lived, and will continue to live on the earth. Hence the problem is, in Nietzsche's words, to determine what type of man we are to cultivate, to Will, as the more valuable, the more worthy of life, and certain of the future, here upon the earth.

The fact that mankind has hitherto been hopelessly divided between the pagan and the religious end, so that every attempt to ensure one future has been frustrated by the attempt to ensure the other –the familiar paradox known as making the best of both worlds– this fact has kept humanity gyrating on its axis. Of progress we have almost lost the meaning. For progress is only to be determined in relation to a goal, and two goals are as bad as none at all.

As a positive human and earthly goal Nietzsche therefore put forward his concept of the Superman; a concept which has become famous and notorious in about equal degree. It is in *Thus Spake Zarathustra* that the outlines of the Superman, as Nietzsche conceived him, may best be seen, and in the portrait of the coming race there sketched we may dimly see Nietzsche's vision. Remembering that Nietzsche denied any purpose in nature other than man's Will, the creation of the Superman may not be left to chance. The modern doctrine of evolution has in this respect misled many people into supposing that men may fold their arms and still progress. Evolve –that is, change from one state to another– they may and must; but evolution is by no means identical with progress. Thus the Superman, if he is to appear at all, must he willed –in plain words, must be bred. The net product of the wills of past humanity –namely, present humanity– Nietzsche could not but regard as inadequate to the demands of the imagination. *'Man is no more than a bridge.'*

As a bridge and a means to an end man is tolerable, but as the end and crown of earth Nietzsche felt that man was contemptible. Hence his scorn for all those who desired to preserve man as he is. Not to preserve man, but to surpass man, was, he said, the aim of the genuine reformer.

The question, however, arises –what type of being is the Superman? Merely to say that he will be as much nobler than man as man is nobler than the ape and the tiger, is to leave a great deal to the imagination. That he will be man, and yet Superman, is clear; but whether he will (or shall –for it is a question of what man shall *will*) be man magnified many times is not so clear. Several writers on Nietzsche (both tacit and avowed) have put forward a Superman differing very little from persons of extraordinary common-sense. Common-sense, we know, is always esoteric ; but the possession of common-sense, even in an extraordinary degree, scarcely divides Superman from man, as man is divided from the tiger.

The truth is, Nietzsche himself found it impossible really to describe the Superman. He could no more foretell what the Superman would be than the Jews could describe their Messiah. The Superman and the Messiah are, in fact, very similar, and it is possible that Nietzsche, in this respect, had borrowed his idea from the Polish Messianist, Juliusz Słowacki. But by means of negatives it was possible for Nietzsche to define what the Superman was not.

To begin with, the Superman, he said, had never existed on earth. The names, therefore, of Cæsar, Napoleon, and the rest are out of court. He did define Napoleon as 'half Superman, half beast,' but we are left in doubt which half of Napoleon was the beast. Then, too, it is safe to say that Nietzsche's coming philosophers, described in *Beyond Good and*

Evil, the Dionysian spirits who shall redeem man, are not themselves Supermen. These he foresaw in a period not very far off, but the Superman may be supposed to lie in a more distant future. Moreover, it is as a preliminary and preparatory race that the philosophers must come.

In humanity, at this moment, there are not only no Supermen, but there is not enough intelligence and Will to make Supermen possible. We have first to develop a caste of mind that shall be qualified to undertake the creation of a superior race. In one sense the Church has been such a caste, with such an end; only, the race it has sought to create is an other worldly race. The Church, said Nietzsche, has always been the arch-traitor of earth.

Finally, there was in Nietzsche's conception of the Superman a good deal of mysticism, with which he himself was scarcely in conscious sympathy. In the opening chapters of *Thus Spake Zarathustra* he describes the three metamorphoses of the spirit, under the names of the Camel, the Lion, and the Child. From his description it is evident that the spirit of man is now only at the Camel stage. Man is a beast of burden. But, as one by one the Camels are laden and go into the solitary desert, they become transformed into Lions. And Nietzsche's description of his coming race of philosophers is as 'laughing Lions.' But the Superman is the Child. In his nature all the wild forces of the Lion are instinctive. He will not seek wisdom, for he will be wise. Man will have become as a little child.

The psychology of these metamorphoses is too profound to be stated here; but nobody who *understands* Nietzsche will doubt that behind all his apparent materialism there was a thoroughly mystical view of the world. As already said, Blake is Nietzsche in English.

It follows from this that the Superman is strictly indefinable. As man is not merely a tiger writ large, so Superman is not merely man writ large. It is probable, indeed, that new faculties, new modes of consciousness, will be needed, as the mystics have always declared; and that the differentiating element of man and Superman will be the possession of these.

But since they are, from the nature of things, unknown except to the few, the task of creating a race such as may *promise* well is all that remains to society. For, in the long-run, it is impossible to divide the powers of the mind from the powers of the body. 'All mind finally becomes visible.' Individually and in a few cases it may be true that noble minds accompany diseased bodies, but the rule is obviously the reverse. Were it not so, the whole of our hygiene, education, even our reason itself, must prove pure delusion.

Hence every end that man conceives for the race must be solidly built on the sensible world.

Whatever the Superman may be psychologically, there is no doubt that physically he must be capable of living on the earth. To create, therefore, a race of men capable of *enjoying* life, capable of entering fully and ever more fully into the life of this earth, such was Nietzsche's proposal. Only by the creation of such a race would the long and bloody toil of hundreds of centuries and countless generations be justified. For when we have praised our famous men, and our fathers that begat us, and have said in our hearts, surely we are the people, and wisdom will perish with us –what, after all, is it? Was it simply for these, for us, that the universe laboured during myriads of years? Are we really the flower, the ultimate blossoming of a Becoming whose stages were marked by the constellations and warmed by solar fires? Was it simply to produce here and there a great man (and him 'human, all too human') amid millions and millions of the mediocre, the dull, the unhappy? Such a thought burned the brain of Nietzsche. With something like the feeling with which we may conceive the Spirit of Humanity beholds us, Nietzsche cried: 'Is this all? Up! Again!'

Though it was only after he been writing for some years that Nietzsche discovered his Superman, his mind had really turned round the conception as its pivot. In the Superman he found the answer to the Dionysian question: How can life be surpassed?

His *Beyond Good and Evil* was a mapping out of the sphere in which the Superman might dwell. And his later works were a continuation of the task he had unconsciously set himself of attacking and destroying the obstacles in the way of Europe's realisation of the Superman.

The justification of Nietzsche's iconoclasm is, indeed, to be sought in this his positive idea. Profoundly and passionately moved by issues which the vast majority are content to ignore, Nietzsche's attack on morality was not simple lust for destruction. So long as the idea of the absolute Good and the absolute Evil prevailed, and men feared to Will lest they should incur the punishment of sin; so long, in fact, as the world was regarded from the priest's standpoint, with innocent causes as sinners, and innocent consequences as executioners, so long was it impossible that men should be persuaded to become responsible for themselves and their future. A super-imposed and tyrannical Good and Evil makes cowards of men, and forbids their saying, '*my* good; *my* bad.'

The substitution, however, of a definite human purpose for a vague indefinable 'divine' purpose, while it destroys morality, really creates a Super-morality. Henceforth it becomes possible to estimate the values of things in precise terms.

'Who keeps one end in view makes all things serve.' And the concept of the Superman, as the goal of human progress, immediately lays the foundation of a scientific revaluation of all the instruments of education.

It was precisely this 'Revaluation of All Values' in the light of the Superman that Nietzsche was beginning when his brain finally gave way. The book in which he was to record his judgements of things, to mark down their values for the coming race, and to provide for Europe a guide, as it were, to the creation of Superman, was also to he his masterwork. It should he his great affirmation, the answer to the problem, that terrible question, with which the tragic Greeks so nobly wrestled: How may life be enabled to become ever and ever more moving, more splendid, more Dionysian? Nietzsche's answer was no other than the Greek answer: by making life more tragic, by the enlargement of the Will of Man –by conflict with gods.

Also available from the Orage Press

Tom Steele

Alfred Orage and the Leeds Arts Club 1893-1923

Dr Tom Steele's seminal study into the first radical modernist art group in Britain, co-founded by Alfred Orage.

ISBN: 978-095445-238-4

Herbert Read

Between the Riccall and the Rye

Poetry and prose writings by Herbert Read on his childhood in Yorkshire and his lifelong yearning to return to the land of his birth.

ISBN: 978-095658-021-4

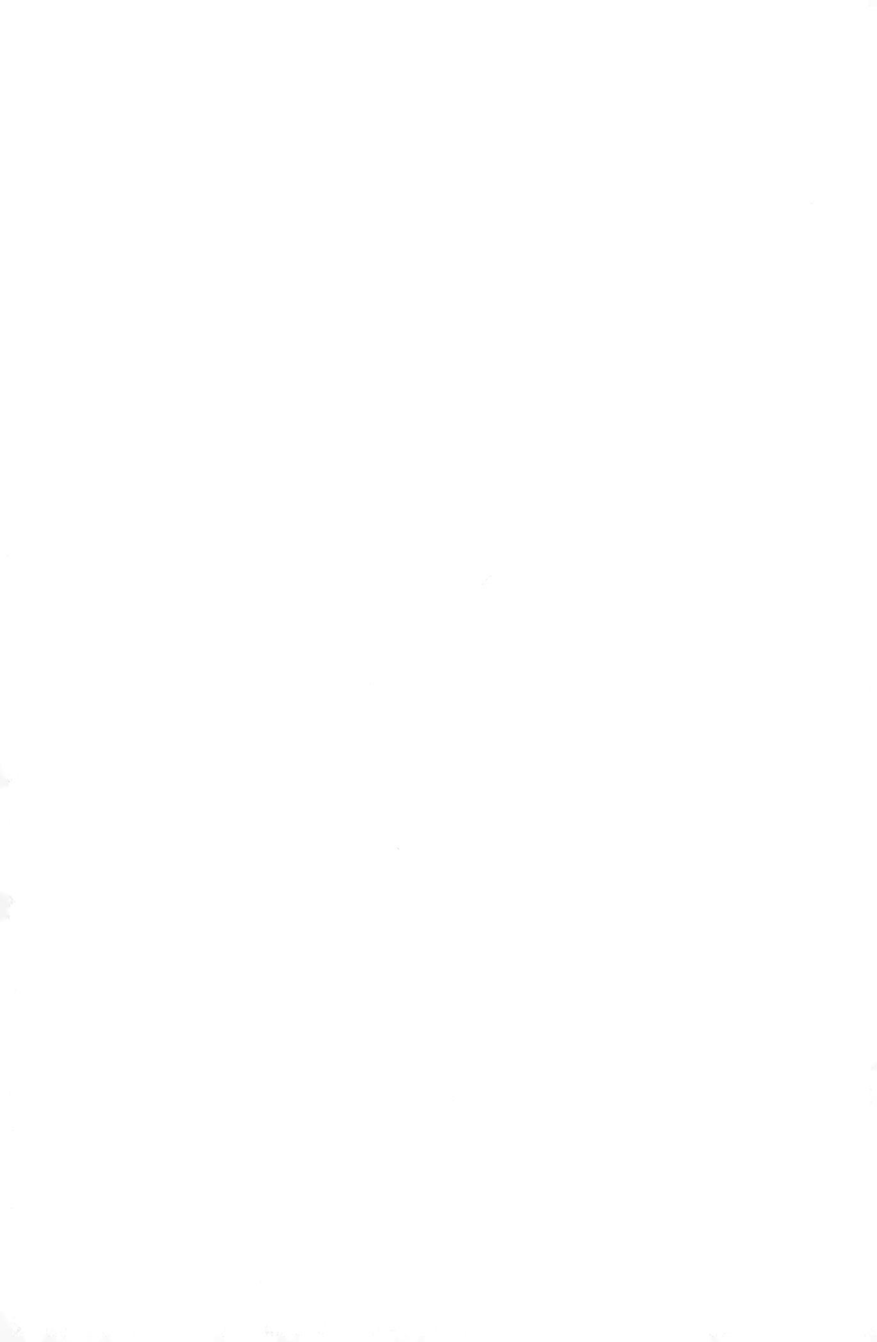

www.ingramcontent.com/pod-product-compliance
Lightning Source LLC
LaVergne TN
LVHW050610100826
845148LV00015B/3210

* 9 7 8 0 9 5 6 5 8 0 2 5 2 *